Piano • Vocal • Guitar

W9-BFX-972

SONGS OF THE 50's
THE DECADE SERIES

Hal Leonard Publishing Corporation

7777 West Bluemound Road P.O. Box 13819 Milwaukee, WI 53213

HAL FRITZ PIANO CO.
ST. MARY'S PA. 834-2764
DuBOIS MALL 371-9443

The Fifties

by Stanley Green

President Dwight D. Eisenhower

Gen. Douglas MacArthur

Bracketed by the Korean War at the beginning of the decade and the increasing American involvement in the Vietnam War at the end, the Fifties are recalled largely as a period of relative tranquility. With the country presided over by the avuncular presence of Dwight D. Eisenhower for eight of the decade's years, it was a time in which people believed in the Power of Positive Thinking, were shocked at the goings on in Peyton Place, and adopted as a symbol of the age the status-seeking, buttoned-down Man in the Grey Flannel Suit. There was also a feeling, reflecting both confidence and relief, that the United States was somehow able to get through crisis after crisis without the cold war turning into a global carnage.

*O*f course, there were serious conflicts and confrontations. The Korean War, which lasted from the summer of 1950 to the summer of 1953 almost involved the country in a full-scale war after Chinese Communist forces had overrun the 38th parallel in an effort to aid the North Koreans. This action resulted in General Douglas MacArthur's threat of massive retaliation which, in turn, resulted in the General's removal by President Harry S. Truman. The Kefauver Senate Committee investigated the farflung activities of organized crime in the full glare of television cameras. NATO — the North Atlantic Treaty Organization — approved a European army to defend the continent against the possibility of a Soviet attack. Senator Joe McCarthy conducted his witch hunt against subversives in government (for which he was later censured by the Senate), thereby introducing the term McCarthyism into the language. Juvenile delinquency — known as "JD" — was on the rise. The Soviet Union sent its tanks into Hungary to quell a rebellion against Communist rule which cost the lives of 32,000 freedom fighters. Racial unrest in the South was accellerated by the Supreme Court's decision that segregated schools were unconstitutional, and federal troops had to be dispatched to Little Rock and other cities.

Frank Sinatra

*T*he decade, however, could be proud of many notable achievements in a variety of fields. Television, which had become the major source of home entertainment in the late Forties, was now available in color and could be transmitted coast to coast. Sir Edmund Hillary and his guide, Tenzing Norkay, were the first to reach the top of Mt. Everest. The Nautilus became the first atom-powered submarine. Dr. Jonas Salk perfected the vaccine against polio. Martin Luther King Jr. led the successful boycott of Montgomery, Alabama. Van Cliburn, of Kilgore, Texas, became the first American to win the Tschaikowsky Prize in the Soviet Union's international piano competition. And the United States launched its first man-made satellite into orbit.

*A*ssorted diversions, fads, scandals, and other pleasures also preoccupied our time. The mambo and the cha-cha brought the Latin beat to the nation's dance halls. Quiz shows abounded on television, and Davy Crockett hats became the rage among youngsters throughout the country. Though the marriage of Grace Kelly of Philadelphia and Prince Rainier of Monaco was unquestionably the wedding of the decade, the period also saw the celebrated knot-tying — and eventual untying — of Frank Sinatra and Ava Gardner, Marilyn Monroe and both Joe DiMaggio and Arthur Miller, Debbie Reynolds and Eddie Fisher, and Elizabeth Taylor and Eddie Fisher.

OLD CAPE COD — WORDS & MUSIC BY CLAIRE ROTHROCK, MILT YAKUS, ALLAN JEFFREY — Featured by PATTI PAGE on MERCURY RECORD NO. 71101 — GEORGE PINCUS & SONS MUSIC CORP. 1650 BROADWAY, NEW YORK, N.Y.

TRUE LOVE — Music and Lyrics by COLE PORTER — M-G-M PRESENTS IN VISTAVISION — Bing CROSBY · Grace KELLY · Frank SINATRA — "HIGH SOCIETY" — CO-STARRING CELESTE HOLM · JOHN LUND · Louis CALHERN · SIDNEY BLACKMER and LOUIS ARMSTRONG AND HIS BAND · JOHN PATRICK · COLE PORTER · CHAPPELL & CO., INC.

*A*s befitting the general mood, the music scene found romantic expressions dominant in the Fifties, whether played by orchestras or sung by balladeers. Most of the instrumental hits, in fact, even featured lush, quasi-symphonic arrangements to decorate such pieces as Leroy Anderson's "Blue Tango," Victor Young's "Around the World" (the composer's theme from the film of the same name), and Hugo Winterhalter's "Canadian Sunset." And then there was the phenomenon known as "mood music."

*B*ut primarily the decade offered a varied collection of soloists singing their hearts out about the joys and pains of requited and unrequited love. Each, of course, had his or her special sound. There was the kittenish purr of Eartha Kitt ("C'est Si Bon"), the roughedged sincerity of Tony Bennett ("Blue Velvet"), the leathery powerhouse of Frankie Laine ("I Believe"), the open-throttled range of Kay Starr ("Wheel of Fortune"), the All-American boyishness of Eddie Fisher ("Oh! My Pa-pa"), the effortless warmth of singing rage Patti Page ("Old Cape Cod"), the high-pitched intensity of Johnny Mathis ("Misty," "Wonderful! Wonderful!"), and the creamy intimacy of Nat "King" Cole ("Unforgettable," "That's All," "When I Fall in Love"). From the movies came two of the nation's favorite girls next door, Doris Day with "Que Sera Sera" (featured in *The Man Who Knew Too Much*) and Debbie Reynolds with "Tammy" (featured in *Tammy and the Bachelor*). And veterans Bing Crosby and Frank Sinatra continued to be in the forefront of our master song stylists. Crosby had a winner in Cole Porter's "True Love" (which he sang in the film *High Society*), and Sinatra had winners in "Three Coins in the Fountain" (which he sang on the film's soundtrack) and "Young at Heart." It should also be noted that the Fifties were awash with lachrymal expressions, notably "Cry" (a Johnnie Ray trademark), "Cry Me a River" (Julie London's first hit), and "Crying in the Chapel."

The earliest indication that changes were about to become evident in the musical taste of the country was the mid-Fifties success of two rock-and-roll items, "Rock Around the Clock" and "Shake, Rattle and Roll," both introduced and popularized by Bill Haley and the Comets. But the singer who most influenced the shape and direction of American pop music was the swivel-hipped, flamboyant Elvis Presley, who won over a new generation to the rockabilly sound of "Blue Suede Shoes," "Don't Be Cruel," "Heartbreak Hotel," and "All Shook Up."

During this period there were also a number of songs — or at least their melodies — that were exhumed from the past. Perhaps the one that went back the farthest was the sentimental ballad "Love Me Tender," another Presley hit, which was known as "Aura Lee" when it was first published in 1861, and later as "Army Blue" when it became a favorite of West Point cadets. "Tom Dooley," the Kingston Trio's chart buster which started a brief vogue for folkish numbers, began life in a North Carolina prison in 1868. There a murderer named Thomas C. Dula penned the threnody about his foul deed, though his name became somewhat altered through the years. "The Glow Worm" dates back to 1902 when, as *"Glühwürmchen,"* it was sung in a German operetta. Its catchy staccato tune made it a perennial barbershop favorite, but it was not until 1952, when aided by a new lyric by Johnny Mercer, that it became one of the Mills Brothers' most requested selections.

Elvis Presley

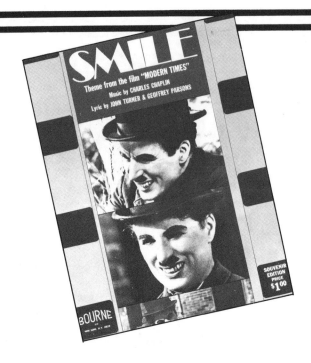

and "They Call the Wind Maria" (pronounced "ma-rī-a"). Then they went on to electrify Broadway with *My Fair Lady,* their acclaimed adaptation of Shaw's *Pygmalion,* whence came the ardent ballad "On the Street Where You Live." Cole Porter was back with *Can-Can,* his next to last big hit, which featured the hymn to the city of lights called "I Love Paris." Prolific composer Jule Styne had two long-run shows in the Fifties. With co-lyricists Betty Comden and Adolph Green he penned *Bells Are Ringing* as a showcase for Judy Holliday to sing, among others, the rueful piece "The Party's Over," and with lyricist Stephen Sondheim he created the songs for the show-business saga *Gypsy,* with Ethel Merman scoring with the pulse-pounding "Everything's Coming Up Roses."

Ethel Merman in "Gypsy"

When "It's All in the Game" was enjoying popularity in the early Fifties, few realized that it had been written in 1912 as an instrumental violin piece called "Melody." Even fewer realized that its composer was Charles G. Dawes, a banker and diplomat, who served as Vice President of the United States under Calvin Coolidge. Charles Chaplin's "Smile," which he composed as the theme for his 1936 silent film *Modern Times,* was another melody that was outfitted with new lyrics in the Fifties and turned into a song hit. It was also in 1936 that the legendary Leadbelly (né Hudder Ledbetter) recorded his "Goodnight, Irene" for the Library of Congress while serving time in the Louisiana State Prison; fourteen years later the Weavers, with Gordon Jenkins' orchestra, made a recording that finally helped it win popular favor. Merle Travis wrote and recorded his cynical protest song "Sixteen Tons" in 1947, then had to wait eight years for Tennessee Ernie Ford to reintroduce it on radio and send it spinning high on the charts.

Songs from Broadway during the Fifties continued to provide the pop music market with some of its most durable standards. The relatively new team of lyricist Alan Jay Lerner and composer Frederick Loewe had their second stage success with *Paint Your Wagon,* a tale of the California gold rush, whose score included "I Talk to the Trees"

And the old masters Rodgers and Hammerstein capped their partnership with *The Sound of Music,* written for Mary Martin. "Climb Ev'ry Mountain" was their inspirational piece that gave courage to the members of the Trapp family as they set out over the Alps to escape the pursuing Nazis.

*T*he serenity of the Fifties, however, was not to last. As the decade came to a close, Americans still seemed optimistic and self-satisfied. But still there was an ongoing problem about what to do about stemming Communist expansion in a tiny country in Southeast Asia. And it showed no signs of being solved . . .

Rodgers & Hammerstein

Mary Martin in
"The Sound Of Music"

ALL I HAVE TO DO IS DREAM

By BOUDLEAUX BRYANT

Moderately

Dream, _____ dream, dream, dream, _ Dream, _____ dream, dream, dream. _ When

I want you in my arms, When I want you and all your charms When
I feel blue in the night, And I need you to hold me tight When

ARRIVEDERCI, ROMA
(Goodbye To Rome)

(From the motion picture "Seven Hills Of Rome")

Words by CARL SIGMAN
Music by R. RASCEL

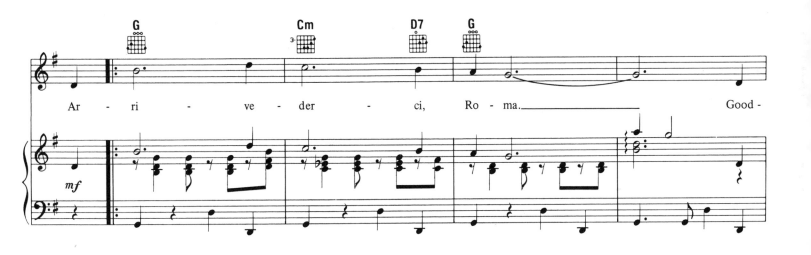

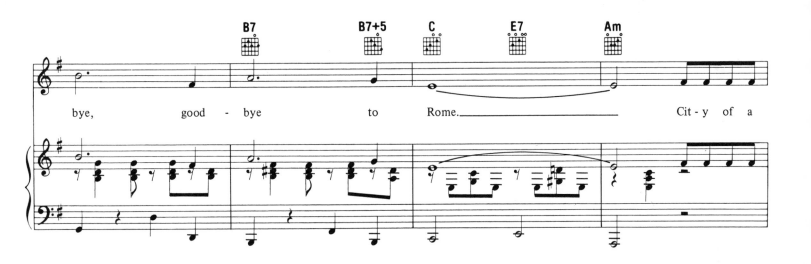

ALL SHOOK UP

Words and Music by OTIS BLACKWELL
and ELVIS PRESLEY

AROUND THE WORLD
(From the Motion Picture "Around The World In 80 Days")

Lyrics by HAROLD ADAMSON
Music by VICTOR YOUNG

AT THE HOP

Words and Music by ARTHUR SINGER,
JOHN MEDORA and DAVID WHITE

Shuffle beat

mf

G6

Ah ah ah ah, Ah ah ah ah,

Em7

Am7

Ah ah ah ah, ah ah ah ah, at the

D7

G6

hop.

G6

Well, you can rock it, you can roll it, do the
swing it, you can groove it, you can

mp - mf

THE BALLAD OF DAVY CROCKETT

(From Walt Disney's Television Production "DAVY CROCKETT")

Words by TOM BLACKBURN
Music by GEORGE BRUNS

Da - vy Crock - ett, lead - in' the pi - o - neer! 19. He
Da - vy Crock - ett, the man who _ don't know fear! 20. His
Da - vy Crock - ett, King of the wild fron - tier!

VERSES

4.
Andy Jackson is our gen'ral's name,
His reg'lar soldiers we'll put to shame,
Them redskin varmints us Volunteers'll tame,
'Cause we got the guns with the sure-fire aim.
Davy — Davy Crockett,
The champion of us all!

5.
Headed back to war from the ol' home place,
But Red Stick was leadin' a merry chase,
Fightin' an' burnin' at a devil's pace
South to the swamps on the Florida Trace.
Davy — Davy Crockett,
Trackin' the redskins down!

6.
Fought single-handed through the Injun War
Till the Creeks was whipped an' peace was in store,
An' while he was handlin' this risky chore,
Made hisself a legend for evermore.
Davy — Davy Crockett,
King of the wild frontier!

7.
He give his word an' he give his hand
That his Injun friends could keep their land,
An' the rest of his life he took the stand
That justice was due every redskin band.
Davy — Davy Crockett,
Holdin' his promise dear!

8.
Home fer the winter with his family,
Happy as squirrels in the ol' gum tree,
Bein' the father he wanted to be,
Close to his boys as the pod an' the pea.
Davy — Davy Crockett,
Holdin' his young 'uns dear!

9.
But the ice went out an' the warm winds came
An' the meltin' snow showed tracks of game,
An' the flowers of Spring filled the woods with flame,
An' all of a sudden life got too tame.
Davy — Davy Crockett,
Headin' on West again!

10.
Off through the woods we're riding' along,
Makin' up yarns an' singin' a song,
He's ringy as a b'ar an' twict as strong,
An' knows he's right 'cause he ain't often wrong.
Davy — Davy Crockett,
The man who don't know fear!

11.
Lookin' fer a place where the air smells clean,
Where the trees is tall an' the grass is green,
Where the fish is fat in an untouched stream,
An' the teemin' woods is a hunter's dream.
Davy — Davy Crockett,
Lookin' fer Paradise!

12.
Now he'd lost his love an' his grief was gall,
In his heart he wanted to leave it all,
An' lose himself in the forests tall,
But he answered instead his country's call.
Davy — Davy Crockett,
Beginnin' his campaign!

13.
Needin' his help they didn't vote blind,
They put in Davy 'cause he was their kind,
Sent up to Nashville the best they could find,
A fightin' spirit an' a thinkin' mind.
Davy — Davy Crockett,
Choice of the whole frontier!

14.
The votes were counted an' he won hands down,
So they sent him off to Washin'ton town
With his best dress suit still his buckskins brown,
A livin' legend of growin' renown.
Davy — Davy Crockett,
The Canebrake Congressman!

15.
He went off to Congress an' served a spell,
Fixin' up the Gover'ment an' laws as well,
Took over Washin'ton so we heered tell
An' patched up the crack in the Liberty Bell.
Davy — Davy Crockett,
Seein' his duty clear!

16.
Him an' his jokes travelled all through the land,
An' his speeches made him friends to beat the band,
His politickin' was their favorite brand
An' everyone wanted to shake his hand.
Davy — Davy Crockett,
Helpin' his legend grow!

17.
He knew when he spoke he sounded the knell
Of his hopes for White House an' fame as well,
But he spoke out strong so hist'ry books tell
An patched up the crack in the Liberty Bell.
Davy — Davy Crockett,
Seein' his duty clear!

BLUE SUEDE SHOES

Words and Music by CARL LEE PERKINS

Bright Tempo (not too fast)

Chorus

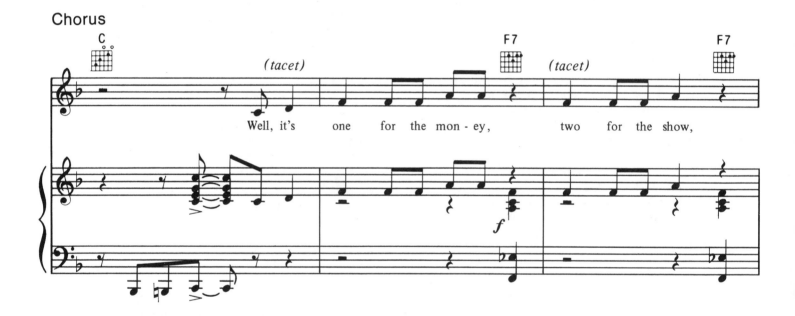

Well, it's one for the mon-ey, two for the show,

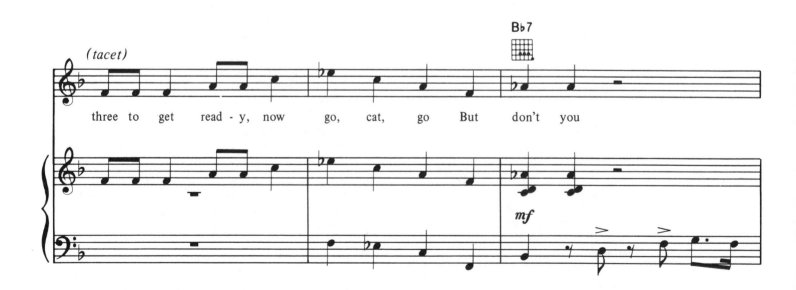

three to get read-y, now go, cat, go But don't you

CANADIAN SUNSET

Music by EDDIE HEYWOOD
Lyrics by NORMAN GIMBEL

BLUE TANGO

Words by MITCHELL PARISH
Music by LEROY ANDERSON

BLUE VELVET

By BERNIE WAYNE
and LEE MORRIS

BYE BYE, LOVE

Words and Music by FELICE BRYANT
and BOUDLEAUX BRYANT

Moderately fast

Lyrics:

There goes my ba - by_____ with some - one new;_____ She sure looks
ro - mance,_____ I'm through with love_____ I'm through with

hap - py;_____ I sure am blue;_____ She was my ba - by_____
count - ing_____ the stars a - bove;_____ And here's the rea - son_____

_____ till he stepped in;_____ Good - bye to ro - mance_____
that I'm so free;_____ My lo - vin' ba - by_____

CARA MIA

Words and Music by
TULIO TRAPANI & LEE LANGE

C'EST SI BON
(It's So Good)

English Words by JERRY SEELEN
French Words by ANDRE HORNEZ
Music by HENRI BETTI

CLIMB EV'RY MOUNTAIN
(From "THE SOUND OF MUSIC")

Words by OSCAR HAMMERSTEIN II
Music by RICHARD RODGERS

CHERRY PINK AND APPLE BLOSSOM WHITE

French Words by JACQUES LARUE
English Words by MACK DAVID
Music by LOUIGUY

CRY

by CHURCHILL KOHLMAN

CRY ME A RIVER

Words and Music by ARTHUR HAMILTON

A la Bach (slightly faster)

I cried a riv-er o-ver you. You drove me,— near-ly drove me out of my head,— While

you__ nev-er shed a tear,___ Re-mem-ber?__ I re-mem-ber all that you said;__

told me love was too ple-be-ian, Told me you were thru with me, an' Now_____ you say you

love me,_____ Well, just to prove you do,_____ Come on, an' Cry__ Me A Riv-er,

Cry__ Me A Riv-er,__ I cried a riv-er o-ver you._____ you.

CRYING IN THE CHAPEL

Words and Music by
ARTIE GLENN

Slowly, with expression

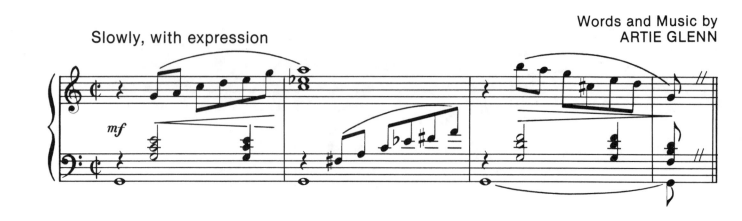

Chorus

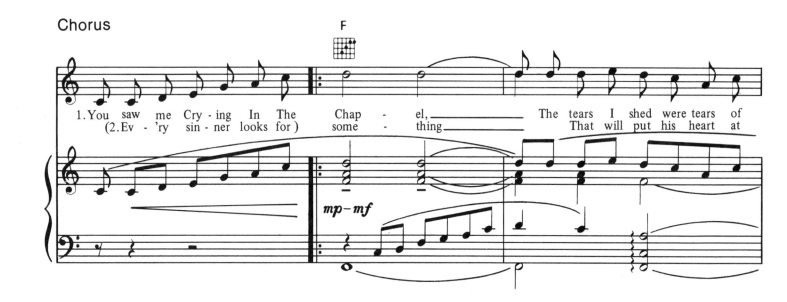

1. You saw me Cry- ing In The Chap- el,_____ The tears I shed were tears of
(2. Ev- 'ry sin- ner looks for) some- thing_____ That will put his heart at

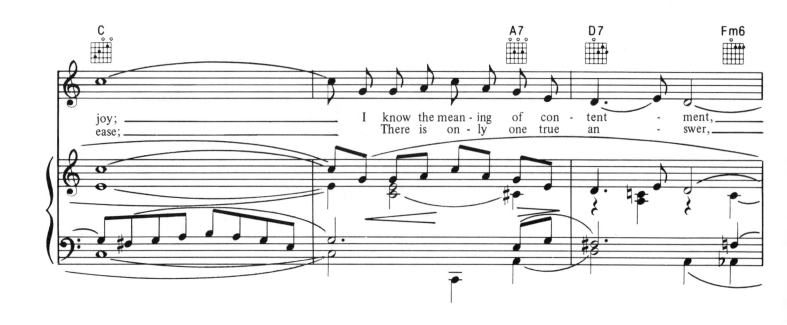

joy;_____ I know the mean- ing of con- tent- ment,_____
ease;_____ There is on- ly one true an- swer,_____

DON'T BE CRUEL
(To A Heart That's True)

Words and Music by OTIS BLACKWELL
and ELVIS PRESLEY

Medium Bright (with a beat)

EVERYTHING'S COMING UP ROSES

(From "GYPSY")

Words by Stephen Sondheim
Music by Jule Styne

FEVER

Words and Music by JOHN DAVENPORT
and EDDIE COOLEY

Verse 3 Romeo loved Juliet,
          Juliet she felt the same,
          When he put his arms around her, he said,
          "Julie, baby you're my flame."

Chorus Thou givest fever, when we kisseth
          Fever with thy flaming youth,
          Fever - I'm afire
          Fever, yea I burn forsooth.

Verse 4 Captain Smith and Pocahantas
          Had a very mad affair,
          When her Daddy tried to kill him, she said,
          "Daddy-o don't you dare."

Chorus Give me fever, with his kisses,
          Fever when he holds me tight.
          Fever - I'm his Missus
          Oh Daddy won't you treat him right.

Verse 5 Now you've listened to my story
          Here's the point that I have made:
          Chicks were born to give you fever
          Be it fahrenheit or centigrade.

Chorus They give you fever when you kiss them,
          Fever if you live and learn.
          Fever - till you sizzle
          What a lovely way to burn.

THE GLOW WORM

Modern Version by JOHNNY MERCER
Original Lyric by LILLA CAYLEY ROBINSON
Music by PAUL LINCKE

THE GREEN DOOR

Words and Music by BOB DAVIE
and MARVIN MOORE

HEARTBREAK HOTEL

By MAE BOREN AXTON,
TOMMY DURDEN and ELVIS PRESLEY

HERE'S THAT RAINY DAY

Words by JOHNNY BURKE
Music by JAMES VAN HEUSEN

I BELIEVE

Words and Music by
ERVIN DRAKE, IRVIN GRAHAM,
JIMMY SHIRL and AL STILLMAN

Moderately (with much expression)

I LOVE PARIS
(From "CAN-CAN")

Words and Music by COLE PORTER

Ev'-ry time I look down on this time - less town, wheth - er blue or grey be her skies, Wheth - er loud be her cheers, or wheth - er soft be her tears, more and

I TALK TO THE TREES
(From "PAINT YOUR WAGON")

Words by ALAN JAY LERNER
Music by FREDERICK LOEWE

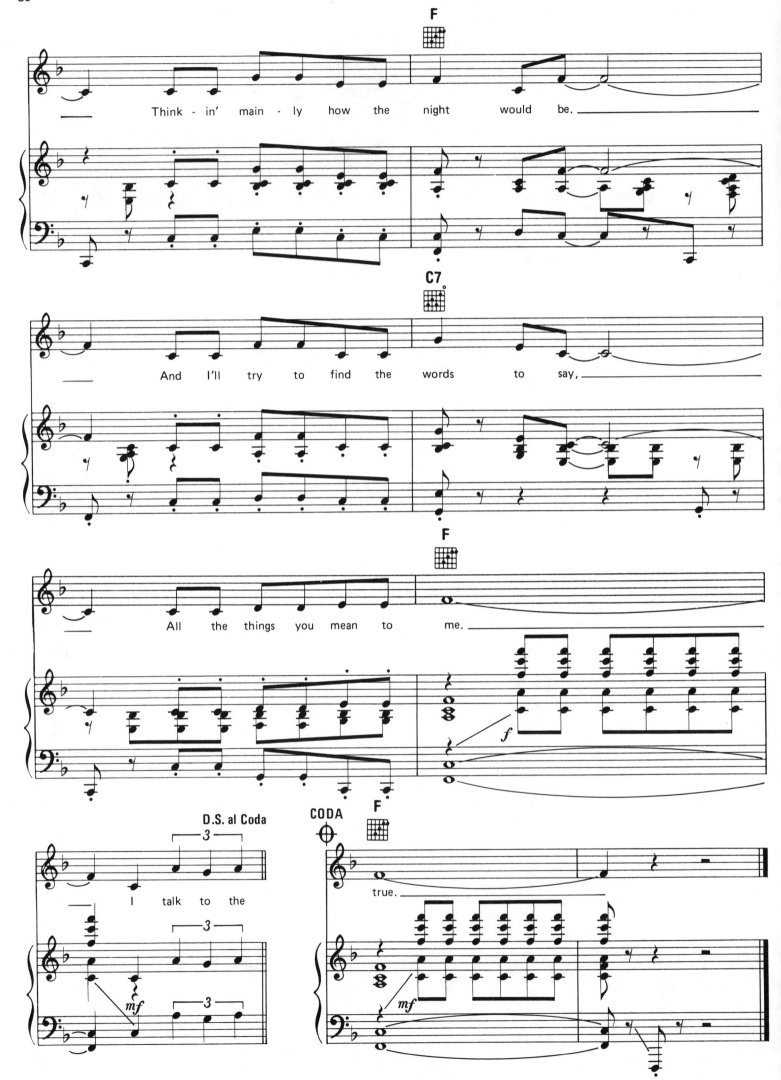

IT'S ALL IN THE GAME

Lyric by Carl Sigman
Music by Charles G. Dawes

Slowly

Man-y a tear has to fall, but it's all in the

game. _____ All in the won-der-ful game that we know as

IT'S JUST A MATTER OF TIME

Words and Music by CLYDE OTIS,
BROOK BENTON and BELFORD HENDRICKS

MISTY

Words by JOHNNY BURKE
Music by ERROLL GARNER

JUST IN TIME
(From "BELLS ARE RINGING")

Words by BETTY COMDEN and ADOLPH GREEN
Music by JULE STYNE

LOVE ME TENDER

Words and Music by
ELVIS PRESLEY & VERA MATSON

Moderately slow

Verse

1. Love Me Ten - der, love me sweet;
2. Love Me Ten - der, love me long;
3. Love Me Ten - der, love me dear;

Nev - er let me go.   You have made my
Take me to your heart.   For it's made there that
Tell me you are mine.   I'll be yours through

EXTRA VERSE 4. When at last my dreams come true,
Darling, this I know:
Happiness will follow you
Everywhere you go.

MR. WONDERFUL
(From the Musical "MR. WONDERFUL")

Words and Music by JERRY BOCK,
LARRY HOLOFCENER and GEORGE WEISS

Slowly and expressively

Why this feel - ing? _____ Why this glow? _____

_____ Why the thrill when you say, "Hel - lo!"? _____

ON THE STREET WHERE YOU LIVE
(From "MY FAIR LADY")

Words by ALAN JAY LERNER
Music by FREDERICK LOEWE

MUSIC! MUSIC! MUSIC!
(Put Another Nickel In)

Words and Music by
BERNIE BAUM and STEPHEN WEISS

OH! MY PA-PA
(O MEIN PAPA)*

English Words by JOHN TURNER and GEOFFREY PARSONS
Music and Original Lyric by PAUL BURKHARD

OLD CAPE COD

Words and Music by CLAIRE ROTHROCK,
MILT YAKUS and ALLAN JEFFREY

Slowly, with expression

ONLY YOU
(And You Alone)

Slowly, with feeling

Words & Music by
BUCK RAM and ANDE RAND

THE PARTY'S OVER

(From "BELLS ARE RINGING")

Words by Betty Comden
and Adolph Green
Music by Jule Styne

QUE SERA, SERA
(WHATEVER WILL BE, WILL BE)

Words and Music by JAY LIVINGSTON
and RAY EVANS

RAG MOP

Words and Music by JOHNNIE LEE WILLS
and DEACON ANDERSON

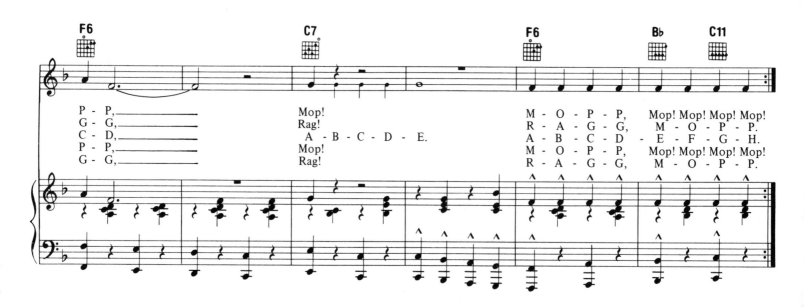

ROCK AROUND THE CLOCK

By MAX C. FREEDMAN
and JIMMY DeKNIGHT

One, two, three o'-clock, four o'-clock rock,

five, six, sev-en o'-clock, eight o'-clock rock, Nine, ten, e-lev-en o'-clock,

twelve o'-clock rock, We're gon-na rock a-round the clock to-night.___

SATIN DOLL

By DUKE ELLINGTON,
JOHNNY MERCER and BILLY STRAYHORN

Medium Swing

Use pedal sparingly

Cig - a - rette hold - er which wigs me

o - ver her should - er, she digs me Out cat - tin'

that sat - in doll.

SHAKE, RATTLE AND ROLL

Words and Music by CHARLES CALHOUN

Moderately Bright

VERSE

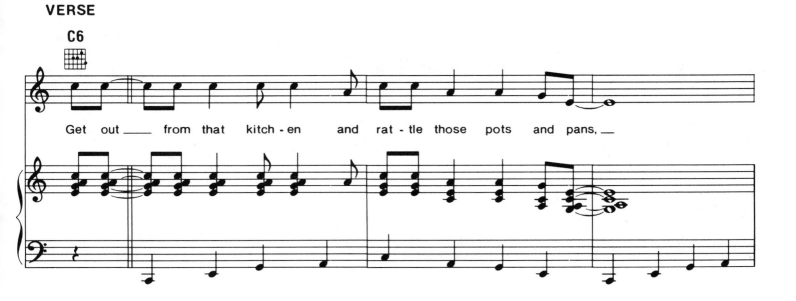

Get out ___ from that kitch-en and rat-tle those pots and pans, ___

Get out ___ from that kitch-en and rat-tle those pots and pans. ___

SH-BOOM
(LIFE COULD BE A DREAM)

Words and Music by JAMES KEYES,
CLAUDE FEASTER, CARL FEASTER,
FLOYD F. McRAE and JAMES EDWARDS

SINGING THE BLUES

Words and Music by MELVIN ENDSLEY

THAT'S ALL

Words and Music by ALAN BRANDT
and BOB HAYMES

SIXTEEN TONS

Words and Music by MERLE TRAVIS

SMILE
(Theme From "MODERN TIMES")

Words by JOHN TURNER & GEOFFREY PARSONS
Music by CHARLES CHAPLIN

Moderately, with great warmth

TAMMY

Words and Music by JAY LIVINGSTON
and RAY EVANS

THEY CALL THE WIND MARIA

(From "PAINT YOUR WAGON")

Words by ALAN JAY LERNER
Music by FREDERICK LOEWE

THREE COINS IN THE FOUNTAIN

Words by SAMMY CAHN
Music by JULE STYNE

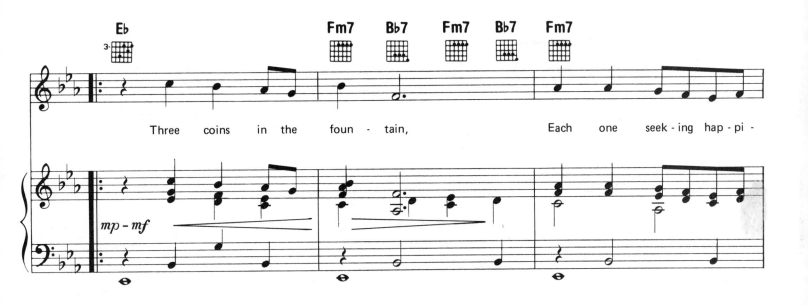

Three coins in the foun-tain, Each one seek-ing hap-pi-

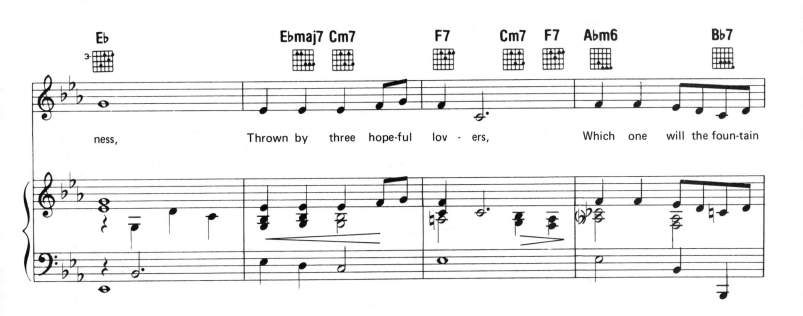

ness, Thrown by three hope-ful lov-ers, Which one will the foun-tain

TOM DOOLEY

Words & Music collected, adapted and arranged by
FRANK WARNER, JOHN A. LOMAX & ALAN LOMAX

Moderately

Hang down your head, Tom Doo - ley, Hang down your head and cry,

Hang down your head, Tom Doo - ley, Poor boy, you're bound__ to die.

I met her on the moun - tain, And there I took her life, I

This time to - mor - row, Reck-on where I'll be? If it

This time to - mor - row, Reck-on where I'll be?

TRUE LOVE

Moderately Slow

Words and Music by
COLE PORTER

UNFORGETTABLE

By IRVING GORDON

Moderately

VAYA CON DIOS
(MAY GOD BE WITH YOU)

Words and Music by LARRY RUSSELL,
INEZ JAMES and BUDDY PEPPER

THE WAYWARD WIND

Words and Music by HERB NEWMAN
and STAN LEBOWSKY

WONDERFUL! WONDERFUL!

Words by BEN RALEIGH
Music by SHERMAN EDWARDS

WHEEL OF FORTUNE

Words and Music by BENNIE BENJAMIN
and GEORGE WEISS

WHEN I FALL IN LOVE

Words by EDWARD HEYMAN
Music by VICTOR YOUNG

YOUNG AT HEART

Words by CAROLYN LEIGH
Music by JOHNNY RICHARDS